Blinders
© Patrick Gabridge
Trade Edition, 2024
ISBN 978-1-934962-22-0

Also Available By Patrick Gabridge

DISTANT NEIGHBORS

Synopsis: A group of suburban neighbors are strangers to each other until an alien space ship crashes into their back yards. After its arrival, they get to know each other a lot better, and faster, than they ever expected (or wanted).

"Distant Neighbors" is a space-age love story about loneliness and longing, and the barriers we set up between us. It looks at the possibility for wonder, not just at the skies and the universe and the thought of unknown life forms, but also at the person living right next door.

Cast Size: 3 Males, 2 Females

BLINDERS
by Patrick Gabridge

For Tracy.

Time: The Present

Place: Various places in America

Character Descriptions: (required: 1 woman, 3 men, 4 chorus members of mixed gender)
Karen Sayer, a reporter, committed to the truth
Stack Thompson, the world's greatest salesman
Chris
Alex

Roles that can be played by a 4 person chorus of mixed gender:
Papergirl
Dr. Cooper Gennette
Reporter1
Reporter2
Tipsy Starlet
Dude
Jolene
Shopper1
Shopper2
Jack--Karen's boss (or Jackie, if you cast role as a woman)
Optometrist
Passerby
Cop
Mailman
Floyd Sayer--Karen's Father
Wanda Sayer--Karen's Mother
Psychologist
Inmates 1-3:
        Carnac
        Miller
        Hideout
Fat Dominic
Wilbur Jenkins (or Wilma if you cast role as a woman)
Senator Caldwell
Voice in Crowd

HOG-1
HOG-2
Moderator
Judy
James

An early version of this play (under the title, *Two Snow-flakes*) opened at the Plays-in-Progress World Premiere Theatre, in Eureka, California, in November, 1998, directed by Michael Thomas. *Blinders* also premiered, that same week at Studio 44, in Denver, directed by Greg Ward.

The first New York production of *Blinders* was produced by the Sage Theatre Company at Raw Space, May 1999.

Director: Frank Calo
Lighting Design: Krista Stella

Cast:
Karen: Nicole Verbois
Stack: Michael D. Kelber
Chris: Phillip Stafford
Alex: Paul Witte
Ensemble/Chorus: Vance Clemente, Tracy Friedman, Michele McKiernan, Jami O'Brien, Jeremy Shepard, and Celeste Wescott.

Special Thanks: Chameleon Stage, Rhombus, the casts, crews, and staffs of the productions and readings by Chameleon Stage, Out of the Blue, Plays-in-Progress, Sage/Spotlight On, Stage Left, Studio 44, and Yellow Taxi Productions. The Karens who worked with me in production: Margaret Casart, Nicole Verbois, Julie Partyka, and Karen Woodward-Massey. The directors who provided so much helpful input: Greg Ward, Frank Calo, Alice Kroman, and Melissa Wentworth. Thanks also to Jessica Maria Tuccelli, Arthur Bracco, and to the Boston Playwrights Theatre. And, as always, thanks to my ever-patient family.

BLINDERS

Scene 1, TWO SNOWFLAKES

(The stage is dark and bare. Props and set pieces are brought on as necessary, with only the barest minimum used to suggest each scene.)

(Spotlight center stage on a young girl hawking newspapers at the top of her lungs.)

PAPERGIRL: EXTRA, EXTRA, READ ALL ABOUT IT! AMAZING DISCOVERY!!! SCIENTISTS DISCOVER TWO IDENTICAL SNOWFLAKES. EXTRA, EXTRA!

(Her spotlight goes black. Another spot comes up on KAREN. KAREN wears a suit, is about thirty-five years old, and carries a steno pad. Her manner is steady and calm.)

KAREN: Two identical flakes of frozen water. That's how it begins. What could be more harmless?

(Karen walks over to a group of REPORTERS and PHOTOGRAPHERS gathered in front of a podium, eagerly taking notes and snapping photographs. DR. COOPER GENNETTE enters.)

GENNETTE: As you are aware, after the first discovery of identical snowflakes ten years ago, my Department of Theoretical Duplication has searched for a set of human duplicates. After years of painstaking research, we are pleased to announce that we have found two people exactly alike. Let me present to you, Chris and Alex.

(Two men walk out, dressed in identical suits. Maybe ALEX is about twenty-five, blond, tall, athletic. Maybe CHRIS is about thirty, dark haired, not tall, and carries a

little more weight than he should. (The important thing is that they should not look at all alike.) They smile and stand next to Gennette for photographs. After sufficient flashes have gone off, they sit in the chairs by the podium.)

GENNETTE: I must admit that we were shocked when we actually found these two marvels of nature. I'd be happy to answer your questions.

REPORTER1: Dr. Gennette, are you sure that Chris and Alex aren't merely identical twins? Perhaps they were separated at birth.

GENNETTE: Any time two people appear identical, our first expectation is twinship. However, in our research with twins we have discovered that the original splitting of the embryo leaves behind a trace marking, a genetic scar, if you will. To answer your question: we are certain that Chris and Alex were not, are not, and never will be... twins.

(A MURMUR runs through the crowd.)

REPORTER2: Are you continuing testing?

GENNETTE: We have already conducted every important test with the most modern scientific instruments. I consider the results one hundred percent verified.

REPORTER1: Rumor has it that you will be nominated for the Nobel Prize. Any comment?

GENNETTE: Everything I've done has been in the name of science. Any recognition is purely secondary.

(Lights cut to black, except for on Karen.)

LOVING PUBLIC

KAREN: Chris and Alex are a smash socially.

(A dazzling young woman with a drink in her hand.)

TIPSY STARLET: Oh, of course I've seen them. They are so cute. I'd love to take one home with me. You can't help wanting to squeeze them, they're so adorable.

(A young guy, DUDE, who shakes as he talks (he's a little strung out.)

DUDE: It's like talking to a fucking mirror, man. Definitely, definitely, I repeat definitely, do not get stoned before going to a party that they're at. It'll pop your circuits. I saw it happen to a guy... Really. He was talking to them, and his head was turning back and forth, back and forth... and the next thing you know he's flopping on the floor like a fish, his eyes rolling up in his head. Scared the shit out of me. I didn't sober up for a week.

(A middle-aged woman in a prim hat enters, perhaps holding a Bible.)

JOLENE: Praise Jesus! The Lord works in mysterious ways. A miracle in our lifetime. Let those secularists talk all they want about science, we know that true wonderment comes from the Lord. The Lord is surely speaking to us at this time, showing all his Glory. Amen, my brothers and sisters. Amen!

(Two SHOPPERS talking together, carrying baskets or bags from trendy shops.)

SHOPPER1: Have you seen their TV commercial?

SHOPPER2: The one for Reebok or the breakfast cereal?

SHOPPER1: The breakfast cereal. I heard they got five million dollars.

SHOPPER2: More for Reebok.

SHOPPER1: Imagine two people exactly the same playing basketball against each other. It'd be impossible.

SHOPPER2: Everyone has good days and bad days.

SHOPPER1: But they have them at the same time. At least that's what I hear.

SHOPPER2: Can you imagine being with them in bed? I mean... you know.

SHOPPER1: You're terrible... What do you think it would be like?

(They exit.)

INTERVIEW

(Karen, alone on the stage.)

KAREN: I am confused, intrigued, irritated. I think that if I can just get an interview, up close and personal, perhaps I'll see what I'm missing.

(Lights up on chairs occupied by ALEX and CHRIS. KAREN joins them.)

KAREN: Thanks for taking the time to talk with me. I'm sure you must be worn out from all the national touring.

CHRIS: Yeah.

ALEX: Pretty much.

CHRIS: But we don't mind sacrificing--

ALEX: --ourselves. It's all for the advancement--

CHRIS: --of science.

KAREN: Do you think the same answers to all my questions?

CHRIS & ALEX: Sure.

KAREN: Do you share emotions, like some twins do? Sort of a telepathy?

ALEX: It's not necessary, since we're exactly the same.

CHRIS: There's no need to share the thoughts, if they're the same in both places at once at the same time.

ALEX: See what we mean?

KAREN: Were you aware of each other before Dr. Gennette found you?

CHRIS: No. We owe all this to Gennette.

KAREN: How did your families take the news? Are either of you married?

ALEX: No.

CHRIS: But you must be.

ALEX: A good looking woman like you.

CHRIS: I didn't know you could win a Pulitzer Prize--

ALEX: --and still be so--

CHRIS: --delicious.

(Dr. COOPER GENNETTE enters and takes a seat.)

GENNETTE: I'm sorry that I'm late.

ALEX: You didn't miss a thing.

CHRIS: We were just getting to know--

ALEX: --the illustrious--

CHRIS: --the luminous--

ALEX: --Ms. Sayer.

KAREN: Yes. Um. Well. Dr. Gennette, the nation seems fascinated with the results of your research. Is this what you expected?

GENNETTE: It's even better. How wonderful to inspire a passion for science. The press has been most cooperative.

KAREN: So I've noticed.

GENNETTE: We present the facts as simply as possible, so they can flow freely to the masses. I'm sure it's difficult for journalists to refrain from commenting. I'm glad they've been willing to trust the Experts.

ALEX: In matters of Science.

CHRIS: And Miracles of Nature.

KAREN: I was wondering... Are you sure all these measurements are correct?

GENNETTE: Every one has been scientifically verified. We have the most advanced instruments in the world. The technology is incredible.

KAREN: I thought this height reading for Alex might be a little optimistic.

ALEX: Excuse me?

KAREN: With all the money poured into the search, I imagine there would be intense pressure to produce a pair of--

GENNETTE: I don't like your tone, Ms. Sayer.

KAREN: You misunderstand.

GENNETTE: Do I?

(The light on GENNETTE fades.)

PRICE TO PAY

(JACK steps towards Karen, flushed with anger.)

JACK: Karen! Are you a scientist?

KAREN: No.

JACK: You don't look like a scientist.

KAREN: I'm not a scientist.

JACK: When I hired you, you didn't tell me you were a scientist.

KAREN: What's your point, Jack?

JACK: A very famous scientist just called to complain about you.

KAREN: I asked a few questions.

14

JACK: Cooper Gennette is impossible to get for an interview.

KAREN: It's my job to ask hard questions.

JACK: Your job was to get face-to-face with the first two identical humans and their discoverer. Your job was to give us an excuse to plaster their incredibly popular faces on our front page, so we can sell newspapers. You used to be my best reporter, Karen. One of the best I've ever known. But this... Why would you do this to me? To yourself? Why are you flushing years of hard work down the toilet?

KAREN: They don't even look alike.

JACK: What?

KAREN: Do they look alike to you?

JACK: Do the scientists say they're identical?

KAREN: Yes, but--

JACK: Did our newspaper say they're identical?

KAREN: We were wrong.

JACK: Do our readers think they're identical?

KAREN: They're idiots.

JACK: Fine. We're all idiots, Karen. We're all wrong. The scientists, the media, the idiots in the streets.

KAREN: That's right.

JACK: Because they don't look alike to you.

KAREN: No, they don't.

JACK: I only need reporters who can see straight. Maybe you'd better get your eyes checked.

(Jack exits.)

VISION

(Karen sits on a chair facing the audience. The OPTOM-ETRIST is a voice over loudspeakers. Perhaps there is a projection of a giant eye.)

OPTOMETRIST: What seems to be the problem?

KAREN: I see things other people don't. Or they see things I don't.

OPTOMETRIST: Headaches? Dizziness?

KAREN: No.

OPTOMETRIST: Double vision?

KAREN: That's the whole problem.

OPTOMETRIST: Hold the paddle over your left eye.

(Blinding light into Karen's face as she holds a plastic paddle over her eye.)

OPTOMETRIST: Look up. Down. Right. Left. Roll it around. Other eye. *(Karen switches eyes.)* Up. Down. Zig zag.

KAREN: Normal?

OPTOMETRIST: So far. I want you to read this.

(An eye chart is projected. It reads something like this:)

A
LEX
ANDCH
RISAREW
ONDERFUL

KAREN: A-L-E-X-A-N-D-C-H-R-I-S... I don't think so.

OPTOMETRIST: No wonder you're having trouble. Which is better, number one or number two?

(SOUND of lenses switching. The chart switches to read:)

I
LOV
ECHRI
SANDALEX

OPTOMETRIST: How's that? Karen? Karen?

(beat. KAREN exits. Lights shift to JOLENE.)

JOLENE: My brothers and sisters in Christ, I know that some of you saw the newspaper articles about our beloved Chris and Alex, degrading them, challenging their unique God-given miraculous duplicity. And I ask you to reach down in your hearts, and pray to God almighty, to smite the purveyors of such lies and filth. Boycott that newspaper. Call your Senator. We must not stand for such immoral attitudes.

(JOLENE exits.)

HOME

(Karen's apartment. KAREN sits on the floor, in the dark.)

(*STACK THOMPSON enters, talking on his cell phone. He possesses a confident charisma. He wears a business suit.*)

STACK: (*into the phone*) No. You're not listening to me. Their product makes customers think their lives will improve. Our product makes them believe. There's a big difference. Exactly. That's what I'm saying. You understand. Perfect. We'll have a contract to you by morning. (*He clicks off his phone, turns on the light, and notices Karen.*) Karen? Why are you sitting in the dark?

KAREN: I have a headache.

(*Stack's cell phone RINGS, but he ignores it.*)

STACK: Sorry.

(*He sits behind her and massages her shoulders.*)

STACK: I thought you were working tonight, big celebrity gala with the wonder twins or something like that.

KAREN: Jack made me take a leave of absence.

STACK: What? Why?

KAREN: The story on the freaks. Gennette and his pals complained, readers complained. Jack thinks I'm losing my mind.

STACK: Jack's a weakling. He forgets that your journalistic integrity is part of the reason why his paper is number one.

KAREN: I don't feel good, Stack. This whole thing, the media reaction, the public reaction, it's making me sick.

STACK: You can't let them get to you. Maybe time off is good.

KAREN: They all treat me like I'm wrong.

STACK: Truth is in the eye of the beholder. Or mouth of the seller.

KAREN: Do they look alike to you?

STACK: You know what you see. It doesn't matter what I think.

KAREN: It matters to me.

(Cell phone RINGS again. Stack ignores it.)

STACK: What I think is that if these jokers had a real marketing guy working for them, the sky would be the limit. Christ, I'd kill to represent these guys. Historical freaks of nature. America loves freaks.

KAREN: Do they look alike?

STACK: I hear that they look alike. My customers can't tell the difference. If the people I sell to think they look the same...

KAREN: You're not selling to me.

STACK: We all sell, all the time. Even to the people we love.

KAREN: So you're never honest with me?

STACK: I'm always honest. Selling is about being honest, about believing what you say. Nobody can sell with a lie. We all need to believe that what we just bought is the God's honest truth.

KAREN: But I believe in concrete truth, factual truth.

STACK: You're a reporter, you should know better.

KAREN: But sometimes, a lot of the time, people listen. They're capable of listening.

STACK: Maybe it'll blow over. You'll be all right.

(He wraps her in his arms.)

KAREN: Do you have to go out tonight?

STACK: I'm supposed to close the deal with SoftMart over dinner. They're downstairs waiting. Do you need me to stay here?

KAREN: No. No. You've been working on this for months. Go.

STACK: Take some aspirin, a long bath, a little Mozart. Try to relax.

KAREN: I'll try.

STACK: You'll be fine. You're tough. Resilient.

KAREN: I am.

STACK: You'll be fine.

KAREN: I will.

(He kisses her and exits.)

KAREN: Good luck! *(to herself)* I'll be fine.

(LIGHTS SHIFT TO:)

ACCUSATION

(COOPER GENNETTE at a podium. CHRIS and ALEX behind him. REPORTERS are watching, joined by KAREN.)

GENNETTE: Due to the tremendous public interest in duplication research, we will expand our testing. In order to find as many duplicate humans as humanly possible, we need a huge number of DNA samples. Our Duplication Vans are roaming the country at this very moment. Due to limited government funding, we ask that our sample volunteers donate a small ten dollar fee.

CHRIS: Please help us with this important scientific research.

ALEX: And get a free Chris and Alex autographed T-shirt.

(KAREN steps in front of her fellow reporters.)

KAREN: What kind of reporters are you people? Open your eyes. These two men don't look a thing alike. Close your ears for a minute and open your eyes.

REPORTER1: Hey, it's Karen Sayer.

REPORTER2: Somebody call security.

REPORTER1: Just can't stay out of the spotlight, huh, Sayer?

KAREN: It's not about me. This is about--

GENNETTE: It's about you constantly attacking my reputation, insulting the other scientists and pundits who agree that our discovery is astounding.

CHRIS: Some people are just afraid--

ALEX: --of change.

CHRIS: And some people--

ALEX: --have an axe to grind.

KAREN: I am not afraid of change. And why would I--

CHRIS: We hoped not to bring this up.

ALEX: But in light of her ridiculous accusations--

CHRIS: --we should help the public understand--

ALEX: --why this might be happening.

GENNETTE: This is not the time.

REPORTER1: We're listening.

KAREN: What are you--

CHRIS: Without turning this into a tabloid explosion--

ALEX: --as you may know--

CHRIS: --we are sometimes--

ALEX: --the objects of curiosity--

CHRIS: --that isn't always--

ALEX: --shall we say--

CHRIS: --pure.

KAREN: Don't even--

CHRIS: Ms. Sayer made a suggestion--

ALEX: --a rather suggestive--

CHRIS: --suggestion--

ALEX: --to put it delicately.

CHRIS: And she was--

ALEX: --rejected--

CHRIS: --dismissed--

ALEX: --in what we thought was a good-natured fashion.

KAREN: I never made a pass at either one of them. You can't make accusations like this. You can't just--

GENNETTE: This press conference is over. Thank you very much, ladies and gentlemen of the almighty press.

KAREN: But they're lying. They're lying! Listen to me! Listen...

(ALL exit.)

(DUDE with a bandage on his forehead.)

DUDE: I didn't really mind getting jabbed too much. It wasn't the first time I'd suffered a blow to the cranial area, if you know what I mean. I looked at the line of hundreds of people all waiting, and I wondered--which one of these things is just like the other?

SPREADING THE TRUTH/TO THE FLAMES

(KAREN enters, holding a stack of papers over her head, shouting. Various PASSERSBY walk in a circle around her, ignoring her. DUDE joins them.)

KAREN: Conclusive proof! Get your proof right here! Page after page of side-by-side photo comparisons. Medical records, weight, coloration, birthmarks. Raw and processed data. Easily digestible. Color pictures.

PASSERBY: Color pictures of Chris and Alex?

KAREN: Color pictures, cute little comic strips. Even a whole section of Chris and Alex jokes.

PASSERBY: Ones they told?

KAREN: About them.

PASSERBY: That's sick.

(The PASSERBY returns to the circle.)

KAREN: These are the actual numbers. See for yourselves. Draw your own conclusions. I'm here to help. Get your data here. Red hot data. Get your data here.

(A COP enters.)

COP: Move on.

KAREN: Officer, would you be interested in a factual expose of our latest celebrity frauds?

COP: You got a permit?

KAREN: These are public sidewalks. I am exerting my First Amendment rights.

COP: Gotta have a permit.

KAREN: I have a right to speak my mind.

COP: You want to put a penny in your pocket, government takes its bite.

KAREN: I'm giving them away, see? Free! Come and get your free debunking guide!

COP: Now you're loitering.

KAREN: I'm--

COP: You're pissing me off.

KAREN: Your happiness is not--

COP: My happiness decides if I bust your skull.

KAREN: But I--

COP: That's it. End of fuse.

(He grabs her and drags her off stage. Her brochures are scattered.)

(CHRIS and ALEX enter as KAREN is dragged off. The PASSERSBY rush to them, pens and papers thrust eagerly. CHRIS and ALEX sign.)

PASSERSBY: Autograph! Autograph! Sign right here. To Edna, Jane, Dallas, Ricky, Adolf, Petruccio, Jimmy, Alice.

ALEX: Do your part for Science.

CHRIS: Volunteer a small amount of DNA.

(The COP re-enters.)

ALEX: A tiny speck of grey matter is all we need.

CHRIS: Keep the rest of the unused mass for yourselves.

ALEX: Only $19.95. A small price to make your mark upon history.

CHRIS: We accept the short, tall, fat, thin, infirm, sane, politicians, serial killers, farmers, watchmakers, tele-marketers. Our sample van is right around the corner. *(CHRIS looks down and sees one of Karen's pamphlets. He picks it up.)* What the hell is this?

COP: Whacko woman was selling them. I made her move on.

ALEX: You'd better find her.

CHRIS: Now!

(COP exits. The PASSERSBY seem tense, uncertain.)

CHRIS: We need lighter fluid.

ALEX: Now!

(The PASSERSBY scatter and exit, searching.)

CHRIS: I will not tolerate people spreading lies.

ALEX: Libel.

CHRIS: Slander.

ALEX: Sedition.

CHRIS: She has no right to attack--

ALEX: --our very nature.

CHRIS: Our celebrity.

ALEX: Our power.

CHRIS: As ordained by science.

ALEX: Sacrilege.

CHRIS: There is only one remedy for such filth.

ALEX: To the flames!

(They exit.)

FASHION STATEMENT

(The two SHOPPERS with their baskets. They have x-shaped bandages in the centers of their foreheads.)

SHOPPER1: I touched one.

SHOPPER2: Liar.

SHOPPER1: He handed me his picture and I stroked his hand.

SHOPPER2: You didn't.

SHOPPER1: I did.

SHOPPER2: And?

SHOPPER1: Wonderful. As soon as I touched him, I went right out and got sampled.

SHOPPER2: Didn't hurt a bit, did it?

SHOPPER1: They say the little scar will be--

SHOPPER2: --a fashion statement. Better than a tattoo. Have you heard anything?

SHOPPER1: Not yet. With my luck it'll be some Chinese woman.

(SHOPPERS exit.)

THE RISING TIDE

(KAREN, in her apartment. She stands face to face with the MAILMAN. He attempts to give her a handful of mail.)

MAILMAN: Here's your mail, Ms. Sayer.

KAREN: Have you looked through it?

MAILMAN: No, Ma'am. That would be an invasion of your privacy. Here you go.

(She won't take it.)

KAREN: Is there a single piece without their pictures or names?

MAILMAN: Excuse me?

KAREN: Chris and Alex.

MAILMAN: They do seem to endorse... I really need to get on with my route.

KAREN: Look through it. I'll take everything that's clean.

MAILMAN: I really--

KAREN: Sort it out, Mailman!

(He fumbles through the mail and finally produces a single envelope.)

MAILMAN: Phone bill.

(She takes it.)

KAREN: Thank you. *(The MAILMAN exits. KAREN sits in her apartment and reads the phone bill.)* This is simplicity. I talk on the phone for a certain number of minutes; I pay a certain amount of money. The money is green. And green is just an agreement to label things consistently. All I want is for the world to be consistent and say that things that are alike are alike and things that are different are different. *(beat)* I really love this phone bill.

(STACK enters, carrying a box and a bag. KAREN does not notice him.)

STACK: Must be quite a phone bill.

KAREN: It was the only thing that wasn't tainted.

STACK: Rough day?

KAREN: I almost got thrown in jail. A screaming mob burned my flyers.

STACK: That's totally the wrong attitude.

KAREN: There's an ugliness behind these creeps, behind the whole bizarre phenomenon.

STACK: It was an isolated incident.

KAREN: The same thing will happen if I try again tomorrow.

STACK: Something must have stirred them up, Karen. People disagree with just about everything in the world, but they don't take action.

KAREN: These did.

STACK: Forget the whole stupid situation. If people want to believe, why not let them?

KAREN: Because it's not true. It's deceit.

STACK: Not true in your eyes. You're stronger, you see better, you're superior to the great mentally unwashed. Forget about the rest of them.

KAREN: I can't.

STACK: It's time to try. I am ready to begin our first evening of complete blockage. We will not turn on the radio, read our mail, or watch the television. We will spend the entire evening with just the two of us.

KAREN: And what about tomorrow?

STACK: Screw tomorrow. Focus on tonight. You and me, together for an evening, without the duplicate specters haunting us. I raided the video store--tonight will be Frank Capra night--"Mr. Deeds Goes to Town," "Mr. Smith Goes to Washington," "It Happened One Night." I will be Clark Gable.

(He hands her the box.)

KAREN: And this is?

STACK: A celebration gift.

KAREN: Celebrating what?

STACK: Our new life of sanctuary together. And one other small thing.

KAREN: Which is?

STACK: Open it first.

(She opens it. It's an evening gown.)

KAREN: Quite the occasion.

STACK: Allow me.

(He dresses her in the dress during the following:)

KAREN: The other news?

STACK: The stage must be set. The moment of the sale, of the final revelation does not come randomly. A seed does not germinate on hard, dry earth. The ground must be plowed, watered, fertilized.

KAREN: You're a master fertilizer, Stack.

STACK: You know what I have, Karen? Faith. I have faith in the ability of the American people to be overcome with desire. Not just wistful longing. I'm talking about lust--lust to be important. A craving to feel that they are more than ants on the sand hill of time. They will pay money to have the magnifying glass pass over them, to make a direct, searing connection between them and the sun. And the whole combination is already in place, the ants, the sun, the glass, but it takes the right person to provide focus, to line things up in just such a way. I'm the right man to do it.

(He finishes dressing her. She's beautiful.)

STACK: *(admiring her)* I am indeed a man of vision. Dinner should be here in twenty minutes. Champagne?

(He produces a bottle and glasses.)

KAREN: It makes me nervous to see you so gleeful.

(STACK pops the cork and pours champagne for both of them.)

STACK: You're nervous because I'm nervous. Nervous, excited, thrilled, worried. I got a new job.

KAREN: Wonderful. What is it?

STACK: Who is the best, most creative, most insightful salesman you know?

KAREN: Stack Thompson.

STACK: You are a veritable Oracle of Delphi.

KAREN: That's my job.

STACK: My job is to satisfy people's hunger. To complete their lives by helping them spend their money to be part of something larger than themselves. I have the opportunity to help people be part of the most influential and popular scientific discovery of our generation.

KAREN: No.

STACK: I understand you might have a few qualms about this job. But I will not bring my work home.

KAREN: You can't do this.

STACK: It's the opportunity of a lifetime.

KAREN: I don't blame you for considering it.

STACK: I love you, Karen. This doesn't change that.

KAREN: It's not just about me, Stack. The entire world is at risk. Help me. Sell the truth.

STACK: I can't sell something people don't want.

KAREN: I've never asked much of you. But I'm asking now.

STACK: We can block it all out.

KAREN: You're too good at what you do. There will be no escape.

STACK: I have to do this, Karen. It's in my nature.

KAREN: Don't say that. I believe a lot of things about you, but I can't believe you would do this.

STACK: Can't you trust my judgment? Just a little.

KAREN: I know what I've seen, Stack. You can't change that.

STACK: I'm taking the job.

KAREN: Get out.

STACK: It doesn't have to be this way. I promise we can avoid--

KAREN: Get out now!

STACK: I won't give up on you, Karen. Never.

(STACK exits.)

FLOYD AND WANDA

(FLOYD and WANDA SAYER in an American Gothic pose, though they wear Chris and Alex T-shirts and he holds a fishing pole, rather than a pitchfork.)

(KAREN enters. FLOYD and WANDA look a little nervous.)

KAREN: Hi, Mom.

WANDA: Karen? Why, don't you look... Floyd! Floyd! Floyd, it's Karen.

FLOYD: Did anyone see her?

WANDA: Why don't you hurry inside, before someone sees you?

KAREN: Stop. Don't touch me. Don't take one more step.

WANDA: What's the matter?

KAREN: Those T-shirts.

WANDA: Aren't they wonderful?

KAREN: Take them off.

FLOYD: We're going to the big rally at the convention center next week.

WANDA: Your dad got us the tickets.

FLOYD: I have connections.

KAREN: Please. Please, please, please take off those T-shirts.

WANDA: Guess which one I'm wearing?

FLOYD: I always put on the wrong one. But your mom's is smaller.

WANDA: Mine is Alex. I just couldn't resist. Everyone will be wearing them. That's half the fun.

FLOYD: Those tickets are impossible to get, unless you have connections.

KAREN: Goodbye.

WANDA: What?

KAREN: I just want a small bit of sanctuary, just for a minute. But you won't take off those DAMN T-shirts!!!

FLOYD: Fine. Don't throw a snit.

(Cardigan sweaters are thrown to Floyd and Wanda from offstage. They put them over their T-shirts. KAREN sits on a stool.)

WANDA: Floyd, she won't eat.

FLOYD: She won't sleep.

WANDA: It is everything I can do to get her in the shower. Clearly there is something wrong...

(FLOYD casts his fishing rod into the air. WANDA exits and enters with a plate of poundcake.)

WANDA: Poundcake?

KAREN: No thanks.

(WANDA exits.)

FLOYD: Oh, yeah. Got a bite. Ease into it. Don't horse it. Fifteen pounds if he's an ounce.

KAREN: You could have gone on your fishing trip, Dad.

FLOYD: Wouldn't think of abandoning my baby.

(WANDA enters with a plate of roast beef.)

WANDA: Roast beef?

KAREN: No thanks.

WANDA: If you don't eat soon, we're going to have to take you to the hospital. And then what will people think? They'll think we starved you, that we were such bad parents that we couldn't even get you to do something simple like eat a slice of roast beef, and they'll think it's no wonder she turned out the way she did, just look at her parents, they can't even get her to eat a slice of blankety-blank bread, let alone control herself around celebrities.

KAREN: I'm sorry if I reflect badly on you in public.

WANDA: I would have thought you finished that "acting out" phase when you dated that boy with the long hair and the motorcycle.

FLOYD: Never liked him.

WANDA: She didn't want you to like him, dear.

FLOYD: I like Stack.

WANDA: What exactly did Stack do? He took an opportunity. Maybe you disagree a little on philosophy. He's a very nice boy.

36

FLOYD: Very promising fisherman.

KAREN: I love Stack, but we're not meant to be together. Is there any other salt you'd like to rub into my wounds? Maybe I should go get a razor and open a vein.

WANDA: It's fine if you want to be melodramatic at home. We're used to it. That's fine.

FLOYD: But don't do it in front of the papers.

KAREN: Chris and Alex don't look alike. They're completely different people.

FLOYD: Talk like that will get us all in a lot of trouble.

KAREN: Then bring it on. Because I'm ready for it. I don't care what your idiot friends say, what my boss says--

FLOYD: You got fired, didn't you?

KAREN: --what Stack says, what you say. It doesn't matter. I will not change my mind.

WANDA: Karen Sayer, act your age. We are alive in the midst of a time of wonder. Stop trying to ruin it.

(KAREN begins a frantic dance around Wanda and Floyd.)

(Karen is joined in her dance by two MEN in white coats, carrying a long strip of cloth. The MEN can be played by Chris and Alex.)

(FLOYD takes a pile of smashed plastic from his pocket.)

FLOYD: Karen!

37

KAREN: Yes, Daddy. Yes, Daddy. Yes, Daddy. Yes, Daddy.

FLOYD: How am I supposed to watch TV without the remote?

WANDA: We'll buy a new one, dear.

FLOYD: She smashed the remote.

KAREN: Yes, Daddy. Yes, Daddy. Yes, Daddy.

WANDA: We'll buy a new one.

FLOYD: SHE SMASHED THE REMOTE!

(KAREN and the MEN in white coats join hands.)

KAREN: Ring around the rosy, pocket full of posies, ashes, ashes, we all fall down.

(WANDA produces a handful of ashes from her pocket and hands them to FLOYD.)

(The MEN in white coats wrap the cloth around KAREN, like a straight-jacket.)

WANDA: Floyd.

FLOYD: No.

WANDA: I thought I hid all the matches from her.

FLOYD: Oh, no.

WANDA: Floyd, honey.

FLOYD: Those tickets were impossible to get. I used my connections.

KAREN (*overlapping*): They are not alike. They don't look alike. They don't sound alike. You all buy whatever they sell you, because you have lost the capacity to use your brains.

WANDA: We have to make the call, Floyd.

FLOYD: Those were hundred dollar tickets. You can't get 'em anywhere. But I have connections.

(The MEN have completely wrapped Karen's arms and upper body with the cloth (so it looks like she's in a straight jacket. The MEN exit with FLOYD and WANDA.)

KAREN: Let me go! There is nothing wrong with me! I am not crazy. I am not crazy. You can't do this to me. I have a right to my opinion. I have a right to disagree. I do not belong here. I do not belong here. You can't make me change my mind. I've seen them, in the flesh. I know the truth. I know the truth. Can't we just agree to disagree? You are all willing dupes, willing to open your pocketbooks and spread your legs. I'm not. We're just different, that's all. I know the truth.

THE PSYCHOLOGIST

(A PSYCHOLOGIST enters on roller skates or riding a scooter. She circles around Karen.)

PSYCHOLOGIST: Are you enjoying your stay at The Institute for Impaired Perception, Katie?

KAREN: Karen.

PSYCHOLOGIST: Excuse me?

KAREN: That's my name.

PSYCHOLOGIST: Are you sure?

KAREN: You can let me go. I'm not a danger to anyone.

PSYCHOLOGIST: Do you know why you're here?

KAREN: My parents had me committed.

PSYCHOLOGIST: Because...

KAREN: I smashed my father's remote control, burned his tickets to see the freaks, and shredded all the news-papers in Tampa County.

PSYCHOLOGIST: And how do you feel about your actions?

KAREN: Happy.

PSYCHOLOGIST: How do you feel about being here?

KAREN: Angry.

PSYCHOLOGIST: And those things are in the wrong order, aren't they? You should feel angry about your actions and happy that someone decided to fix your problem.

KAREN: I don't have a problem.

PSYCHOLOGIST: Let's take a little test, shall we? Tell me the first word that comes to mind when you see these pictures.

(The PSYCHOLOGIST activates slides projected onto the rear wall. The first slide is of a horrific demon.)

KAREN: Satan.

PSYCHOLOGIST: And this?

(Picture of Hitler.)

KAREN: Hitler.

(Picture of Saddam Hussein.)

KAREN: Hussein.

(Picture of Chris.)

KAREN: Fake. Impostor. Evil incarnate. Chris.

PSYCHOLOGIST: Hmmm.

(Picture of Alex.)

KAREN: Scum sucking parasite. Alex.

PSYCHOLOGIST: You're sure it's not Chris?

KAREN: Absolutely.

PSYCHOLOGIST: Because?

KAREN: They look different.

PSYCHOLOGIST: What if I told you they were the same picture?

KAREN: You'd be lying.

PSYCHOLOGIST: What if I told you they were all the same picture?

KAREN: You should get your eyes checked.

PSYCHOLOGIST: So this picture--*(Satan image)*--and this image--*(Chris image)* --appear to be?

KAREN: Different visually, identical thematically.

PSYCHOLOGIST: Very interesting.

KAREN: This doesn't make me dangerous. Please. I just want to go. I won't bother anyone.

PSYCHOLOGIST: We'll start your treatment on Tuesday.

KAREN: My treatment? What is my treatment?

(The PSYCHOLOGIST wheels off.)

VISITATION

(MILLER crawls across the floor, tapping a red poker chip. HIDEOUT sits in the corner, maybe drooling a little. A pile of oversized red poker chips sits in front of him. STACK enters, kisses KAREN, and unwraps the cloth that binds her.)

KAREN: Hi.

STACK: They made me check my pager and cell phone at the door.

KAREN: Loud noises set some people off.

STACK: It makes me uncomfortable. *(nods towards Miller)* What's he in here for?

KAREN: He can't tell the difference between Lite beer and regular.

STACK: Maybe this place isn't so bad. *(beat)* So, have they helped you?

KAREN: They're still working on me.

STACK: They have no idea how stubborn you are.

KAREN: How are things on the outside?

STACK: Oh, you know.

KAREN: Crazy.

STACK: New job's going gangbusters.

KAREN: You're the best.

STACK: I play with oversaturation like a research chemist.

KAREN: But you always go too far.

STACK: My big triumph takes place tonight. You shouldn't watch.

KAREN: Maybe you should just tell me.

STACK: It's a secret.

KAREN: Who am I going to tell?

STACK: This is really quite a place. Pastel walls, soft lighting. Very soothing. Soft music playing in the halls.

KAREN: They're trying aversion therapy on me. It's not working.

STACK: People would pay good money to come here. Nice view. First rate gardens, no phone calls, complete isolation. First we need to get rid of the stigma of staying in a nut house. Get a few celebs to visit. All the best writers and thinkers went insane at one time or another. We can give it a certain yuppy literary cachet. "Open yourself to whole new ways of thinking."

KAREN: Don't you miss me at all?

STACK: It's driving me crazy. I think about you all the time. I worry about how they're treating you, I worry about... I've never met anyone like you, Karen. I never will.

KAREN: Get me out of here, Stack.

STACK: You can get yourself out. It's simple. All you have to do is say they look the same.

KAREN: They look the same... and I love them, because they are the pure, adorable, identical direct descendants of some power on high that has decided to create these two wonders of the world. I love them and will buy every fucking video, poster, postage stamp, T-shirt, seat cushion, salt shaker that features their goddamned graven images. If I do that, I will be considered safe and allowed to venture back into the world.

STACK: I hear what you're saying. But if you cooperate, just a little--

KAREN: If I learn to do it once, I'll do it again. And again and again and again and again. Constant renunciation of my eyes and brain. Now, that seems dangerous.

STACK: You know what? You're absolutely right. The bare bones truth: this is the best place for you right now. If you go outside, you will be bombarded by the faces, voices, and personalities of my two charges. And once that happens, you will go insane.

KAREN: So I'm supposed to hide in here while you turn the world upside down.

STACK: Just until I've emptied all the change from its pockets. (*looks at his watch*) I have to run.

KAREN: Come again, please.

STACK: I'll be back next week, I promise.

(They kiss. For a moment, STACK appears uncertain.)

STACK: *(whispers)* I'll see what I can do.

(He runs off stage.)

ANNOUNCEMENT

(CHRIS and ALEX approach a podium (they're speaking on television--you can place them behind an oversized TV frame if you like. The lights of a thousand flash bulbs go off. Various images will be projected behind them. First: a U.S. flag. On the opposite side of the stage (in the asylum), CARNAC, MILLER, HIDEOUT (who hasn't moved) and KAREN watch the Duplicates on TV.)

CHRIS: Most esteemed ladies and gentlemen of the all-knowing--

ALEX: --all comprehending press corps.

CHRIS: And also citizens and citizenettes of the United States of America, the best country in the world.

(Thunderous applause.)

ALEX: As Duplicates, we have enjoyed a tremendous outpouring of support, fan mail, gifts, offers of sexual favors.

CHRIS: Which were all turned down.

ALEX: As near as we can remember.

CHRIS: After being discovered, your response has allowed us to see this entire great country. From Augusta, Maine, to Augusta, Georgia.

(Slide of the ocean)

ALEX: From sea to shining sea.

(Slide of mountains)

CHRIS: O'er purple mountains majesty.

(Slide of wheat fields)

ALEX: And amber waves of grain.

CHRIS: And what we've sensed above all--

ALEX: --is a deep sense of abiding hope.

CHRIS: That you the press--

ALEX: --and you the people--

CHRIS: --are waiting for the right person--

ALEX: --or people--

CHRIS: --to come along and unite this great country.

ALEX: We need a leader--

CHRIS: --or leaders--

ALEX: --to show the way.

CHRIS: So Alex and I decided,

ALEX: At the same time,

CHRIS: Naturally,

ALEX: That it was time for us to step forward.

CHRIS: Tonight, we are ready to announce to the press--

ALEX: --and to the world--

CHRIS: --and even to the public--

ALEX: That we will seek the office of the President of the United States of America,

CHRIS: To seize upon hope--

ALEX: --to make dreams come real,

CHRIS: Because two heads are better than one.

(Slide of Chris and Alex with large slogan: "Two Heads Are Better Than One.")

ALEX: We will be doubly able to serve the press and people of the United States because we have twice the energy, twice the presence of any single person.

CHRIS: Thank you. And remember...

ALEX & CHRIS: TWO HEADS ARE BETTER THAN ONE.

ALEX: Good night.

CHRIS: God Bless America.

(CHRIS and ALEX exit.)

(The INMATES applaud.)

MILLER: Two heads are better than one. Damn straight. And will they make your whites whiter? Will they make your brights brighter? Damn straight.

CARNAC: Those guys fascinate me. When I read their minds, it's like I'm looking inside one single, giant head.

MILLER: See, people like that, they don't care about Lite Beer. They don't condemn a person for being different. Where's my absentee ballot?

CARNAC: My lawyer says I should be able to vote once for each personality.

MILLER: Eight more votes for Chris and Alex. Amen. The world needs more people like you, Carnac.

CARNAC: Karen still thinks the whole world is full of shit.

MILLER: The world needs a lot less people like her. Hell, this asylum needs less people like her. Whole place is going down the shitter.

MILLER & CARNAC: *(chanting)* Chris and Alex. Chris and Alex. Chris and Alex. Chris and Alex.

(MILLER and CARNAC exit, chanting and dancing.)

HIDEOUT: Country's full of 'em.

KAREN: Did you speak? I thought you were catatonic.

HIDEOUT: Don't believe everything you see. I'm not crazy.

KAREN: Neither am I.

HIDEOUT: And those two phonies don't look a thing alike.

KAREN: What?

HIDEOUT: Different as Italians from Sicilians.

KAREN: You believe me?

HIDEOUT: I believe my own eyes more than any bullshit that gets fed to me.

KAREN: So I'm not crazy.

(HIDEOUT produces a red poker chip.)

HIDEOUT: Red or blue?

KAREN: Red.

HIDEOUT: One of us is crazy. (*HIDEOUT tosses KAREN the poker chip.*) Go to the Blue Wing. The mesh on the third window from the end is loose. Use that chip to pry up the last two strands. The watchmen change at 9:30.

KAREN: How did you know--

HIDEOUT: We've been watching you. Get to Newark, 32nd and Cherry, Garden State Lanes. Find Fat Dominic and tell him that Elmer said to lend you his shoes.

KAREN: Elmer?

HIDEOUT: It's my, uh, code name. Dominic will set you up with a piece.

KAREN: A gun?

HIDEOUT: We'll get you access. You do the rest. Keep your mouth shut and your hands steady. Good luck, Fruit Loops.

(HIDEOUT exits.)

(KAREN examines the poker chip and exits.)

END OF ACT I.

Act II, scene 1, THE DREAM

(KAREN, center, back to the audience, her arms hang loosely by her sides, like a gunfighter. A holster with a gun is strapped to her hip.)

(CHRIS and ALEX enter in a blare of triumphant music--Hail to the Chief(s)--and stand in front of matching podiums. They wave happily to an unseen audience.)

CHRIS: Thank you.

ALEX: You're too kind.

CHRIS: Too kind. We have two pieces of excellent news to share this evening with the press--

ALEX: --the world--

CHRIS: --and even you the people.

ALEX: The results of our exhaustive research are finally in.

CHRIS: The response from all of you was tremendous.

ALEX: Even after we raised the price to forty-five dollars,

CHRIS: The samples just kept pouring in.

ALEX: And it paid off.

(Two people enter, dressed exactly like Chris and Alex.)

CHRIS: Dr. Gennette has discovered two more people exactly like me and Alex.

ALEX: Please give a warm welcome for Davis Malcomsen, former head of General Motors.

CHRIS: And Barry Levy, former program director for Worldwide Cable Network.

ALEX: Since they have shared our exact molecular make-up since birth.

CHRIS: We will add them to the Presidency immediately.

ALEX: Four heads are better than one.

CHRIS: This will only enhance our ability to continue ruling America--

ALEX: --with a velvet glove--

CHRIS: --over our iron fists--

ALEX: --grasping for what belongs to us:

CHRIS: Your hearts.

ALEX: Your minds.

CHRIS: Your pocketbooks.

ALEX: Your firstborn.

CHRIS: And if that wasn't good enough,

ALEX: The College of Cardinals has finally returned its verdict.

CHRIS: Give a warm welcome to popes--

ALEX: --Alex, Barry, Chris, and Davis the First. God himself--

CHRIS: --has ordained our fate--

ALEX: --and you will fall at our feet--

CHRIS: --and kiss our rings.

ALEX: Assume the position, world.

CHRIS: And you, too, press corps.

ALEX: And all you loyal followers.

CHRIS: If your neighbor waivers,

ALEX: If he quavers,

CHRIS: If he shudders at the thought,

ALEX: There is no place for him--

CHRIS: --in the world.

ALEX: Amen, brother.

CHRIS: Amen.

(KAREN draws her gun and fires. All four duplicates fall and crawl off stage. She turns to face the audience, covered in blood.)

KAREN: The dream barely leaves me, even when I'm awake. I can feel the gun--its weight, its cool, soothing barrel. The handle fits perfectly into my palm. Its sound is pure joy, ripping away the oppression of an entire world with four perfectly placed lead slugs.

(KAREN exits.)

(DUDE dressed in red, white, and blue, and covered in Chris and Alex stickers. He still has band-aids on his forehead.)

DUDE: I'm not the only one, Man. There are thousands of us. We just follow them wherever they go. A great big rolling happy family, stuck in absolute wonder and amazement at our two identical brothers. There's lots of things I'm not sure about in life. Global warming, eating meat, drinking water, the morality of a world-wide capitalist economy, but I'm sure these dudes are cool. For once in my life, I'm gonna vote. (*laughs*) Move over Mom and Dad, I am America!

GARDEN STATE LANES

(*A thin man behind a counter, FAT DOMINIC, polishes bowling shoes. SOUNDS of bowling.*)

(*KAREN enters, bedraggled, nervous.*)

FAT DOMINIC: Can I help you?

KAREN: I'm looking for Fat Dominic.

FAT DOMINIC: That's me.

KAREN: Elmer sent me. He said I could borrow his shoes.

FAT DOMINIC: You seen Elmer?

KAREN: He said you should let me borrow his shoes.

FAT DOMINIC: Where is he?

KAREN: Can't say.

FAT DOMINIC: How do I--

(*KAREN leans across the counter and grabs DOMINIC by the lapels.*)

KAREN: Give me the shoes, Dominic.

FAT DOMINIC: Okay, okay. Let me go.

(She lets him go. He straightens himself out.)

FAT DOMINIC: You got the blue chip?

(KAREN pulls the red poker chip out of her pocket and hands it to DOMINIC.)

FAT DOMINIC: You're the real thing, all right.

(DOMINIC reaches under the counter and produces a large pair of bowling shoes. KAREN reaches inside.)

FAT DOMINIC: Not here. Go to lane 24. There's someone waiting for you.

KAREN: Who?

FAT DOMINIC: It's a friend.

(DOMINIC exits. WILBUR JENKINS, enters, wearing a trenchcoat and fedora festooned with Chris and Alex stickers. He holds a bowling ball and seems to be prepar- ing to bowl. KAREN sits on a chair nearby and feels in- side the shoes. She produces a small handgun.)

WILBUR: Keep that out of sight!

(KAREN shoves the gun into her pocket.)

KAREN: Do I know you?

WILBUR: Don't look at me. Don't look at me. Start
bowling. Get a ball.

(KAREN gets a bowling ball. Both of them concentrate on their balls and don't look at each other.)

KAREN: Dominic says you're my friend.

WILBUR: Elmer thought we might be able to help you.

KAREN: We?

WILBUR: T.U.M.O.T.S.C.A.F.R.O.P.

KAREN: Excuse me?

WILBUR: The Underground Movement Operating To Stop Chris and Alex From Ruling Our Planet. T.U.M.O.T.S.C.A.F.R.O.P.

KAREN: How do you know so much about me?

WILBUR: You're our Messiah. We have a secret network of hundreds who refuse to fall under their spell, who trust their own eyes.

KAREN: What do you want from me?

WILBUR: We know of your quest.

KAREN: What I plan to do is illegal, possibly immoral, and definitely unpopular.

(WILBUR reaches under his coat and produces a large manila envelope. He tosses it at her feet.)

WILBUR: That is their itinerary for the next two weeks. Names and backgrounds of their security staff. New identity papers. A press pass.

KAREN: You're going to make me go through with this.

WILBUR: I'll make sure you get an opportunity. I can't provide you with courage.

KAREN: What's your name, Mr. Tumotscasfrop?

WILBUR: Wilbur.

KAREN: I'm not always sure of myself, Wilbur. And I'm definitely not sure about you.

WILBUR: I'll meet you in the parking lot. Look for a green Yugo.

(WILBUR exits.)

KAREN: The gun isn't anything at all like in my nightmare. It's oily, dirty, heavy, uncomfortable. Completely foreign. It saps my righteousness with the power of filthy reality. (*beat*) I will be carried to my fate in a green Yugo.

(KAREN exits.)

DRIVING RANGE

(A strip of green indoor/outdoor carpeting unrolls across the stage. CHRIS and ALEX enter with golf clubs in their hands and begin swinging. STACK stands nearby and looks worried.)

CHRIS: FORE!

ALEX: You don't have to yell fore--

CHRIS: -at the driving range. I know.

ALEX: Of course.

CHRIS: FORE!

STACK: What are we going to do?

ALEX: Karen Sayer is a crackpot.

CHRIS: A loony.

ALEX: No one will--

CHRIS: --listen. No one listens.

STACK: The doctors said she could be dangerous.

CHRIS: That's why we have--

ALEX: --the Secret Service.

CHRIS: Constant vigilance.

ALEX: I can barely take a piss--

CHRIS: --without one peering over a shoulder.

ALEX: That's where I draw the line.

CHRIS: Nervous bladder.

STACK: Karen can be very resourceful.

CHRIS: FORE!

ALEX: So can we.

CHRIS: We know how--

ALEX: --busy you are.

CHRIS: So we took the initiative.

ALEX: Proactivated ourselves.

STACK: You what?

ALEX: We're taping a public service announcement--

CHRIS: --tomorrow--

ALEX: --with the FBI.

CHRIS: Karen Sayer's face will be plastered--

ALEX: --smeared--

CHRIS: --exposed on every TV across the nation.

ALEX: And with a hundred million loyal--

CHRIS: fans

ALEX: worshippers

CHRIS: zealots

ALEX: She'd better hope the police catch her first.

CHRIS: FORE!

STACK: But... but... you can't, you... you have a very busy schedule tomorrow. No, if they... She would be... There's no possibility--

CHRIS: Stack.

ALEX: We're talking about our safety.

CHRIS: Priorities.

ALEX: Priorities are everything.

STACK: I'm concerned about your safety, of course, but--

CHRIS: I'm getting the hang of this golf thing. Who would have thought the key to politics is a good suit and a decent golf swing?

(SENATOR CALDWELL enters with a golf club and begins swinging.)

CHRIS: I thought this course was--

ALEX: --private--

CHRIS: --exclusive.

ALEX: Since when did they admit--

CHRIS: --pond scum?

STACK: Hello, Senator Caldwell.

SENATOR CALDWELL: The Dynamic Duo and their puppet master.

CHRIS: Bite me.

ALEX: Go choke on your own vomit, old man.

STACK: What do you want, Caldwell?

SENATOR CALDWELL: I just wanted to get near the Mega Celebrities, to be bathed in the golden glow of their presence.

CHRIS: He's not all that bad.

ALEX: We can make allowances--

CHRIS: --for flattery.

STACK: Shouldn't you be practicing for next month's debate?

SENATOR CALDWELL: That's precisely why I'm here.

CHRIS: What about our golden glow?

ALEX: Did you want an autograph?

SENATOR CALDWELL: I have the ability to tamper with your landslide, Stack.

ALEX: We will crush you.

CHRIS: Bury you.

ALEX: Destroy you.

CHRIS: FORE!

SENATOR CALDWELL: Damage can always be done. Rumors, photos--

STACK: My clients are Teflon coated.

SENATOR CALDWELL: If Karen Sayer gets to them, who knows what she might do. I hear she escaped.

CHRIS: Our followers will find her--

ALEX: --and tear her from limb to limb.

CHRIS: And grind her bones--

ALEX: --to make our bread.

SENATOR CALDWELL: Unless she has help.

STACK: What do you want?

SENATOR CALDWELL: My consolation prize for being robbed of the presidency by a pair of freaks.

(STACK restrains CHRIS and ALEX.)

CHRIS: Freak!

ALEX: Want to see what a freak can do--

CHRIS: --to your sorry ass?

STACK: Sit. Stay. Quiet.

(They obey.)

SENATOR CALDWELL: My price is very reasonable.

STACK: You repulsive toad. You think I haven't heard from every two-bit, half-witted shakedown artist in the country? I have what America wants, not you. Extend your rattling cup elsewhere, because America will not hear you.

SENATOR CALDWELL: You are destroying the system, Stack. MY system. Sabotaging America's machinery, perverting everything I've stood for. Even someone like me believes in something. My colleagues and I have made our fortunes, and even done some good in the world. You want to eradicate not just our way of life, but our very selves. I will not be annihilated. Do you understand me? Don't push me too far.

(CALDWELL exits.)

ALEX: Oooh. He seems a little stressed.

CHRIS: Poor loser.

ALEX: Well said, Stack.

CHRIS: Good show.

ALL: FORE!

(ALL exit.)

FLOYD AND WANDA MEET THE FBI

(FLOYD and WANDA sit uncomfortably in chairs in their home.)

FLOYD: We're so sorry that you're here, Special Agent Fluffenbecker. None of this, well it's just not like our daughter. Not at all.

WANDA: Floyd said that you wanted some pictures of Karen. I don't have anything recent, but I do have some pretty ones. This is from her Junior Prom. Wasn't she something?

FLOYD: She's a spitfire, but she wouldn't hurt a soul. Especially not Chris and Alex.

WANDA: This is from the Junior League Mother-Daughter Tea. I always thought she looked nice in pink. I never told her that, of course, because if I did, then I'd never see her wear it again. I told her she looked good in green. *(whispers)* She looks horrible in green.

FLOYD: I hope you find her soon, Agent Fluffenbecker, because we're a heap of worried about her. People have been saying things on the talk radio about what they'd do to her if they...

WANDA: Here's her sweet sixteen, with her new bicycle. She didn't want a car, on account of the pollution. She's thoughtful that way. She thinks about things, see?

63

FLOYD: Not that I blame folks for being upset. And if she ever did try to assassinate Chris and Alex, well that might be... But, look, we don't want Karen hurt, not like that.

(Lights out on FLOYD and WANDA.)

OPPORTUNITY

(Two empty podiums. Enormous crowd projected onto the rear screen. KAREN stands not far from the podium, hands thrust into her raincoat. She is surrounded by a cardboard cutout crowd.)

(STACK suddenly appears at a podium.)

STACK: Ladies and gentlemen. It is time for the moment you've been waiting for. It is time for the split second that will change your reason for existence. Those of you who have been lost, have found a home. Tonight, you will all become part of what is the biggest movement in America. Tonight, YOU WILL BE PART OF CHRIS AND ALEX!

(Deafening applause and cheering. CHRIS and ALEX emerge, in their trademark matching suits, and shake hands with Stack.)

ALEX: Thank you, Stack.

CHRIS: And thanks to all of you--

ALEX: --for coming to listen--

CHRIS: --and to share--

ALEX: --what we think is important.

(Thunderous cheering.)

ALEX: Because what we think is important--

CHRIS: --is what you think is important.

ALEX: And that's why you can trust us to lead you,

CHRIS: To lead America,

ALEX: Wherever we want it to go.

(Loud cheers.)

ALEX: You may have seen some press conferences lately where reporters have asked what exactly do we stand for.

CHRIS: Questioning our programs.

VOICE IN CROWD: Lynch 'em!

ALEX: No, no.

CHRIS: Reporters are our friends. Some are even here tonight.

(They wave and smile. Thousands of flash bulbs go off.)

ALEX: Stop.

(Flash bulbs stop.)

CHRIS: We want people to know that we're not afraid of hard questions.

ALEX: Of tough decisions.

CHRIS: Of making whatever choices we feel we have to.

ALEX: No matter how popular they may be.

CHRIS: What do we stand for?

ALEX: We'll tell you.

CHRIS: Lower taxes.

(Loud cheers.)

ALEX: Better schools.

(The cheering rises and falls throughout the following, but gradually builds and builds.)

CHRIS: Free lunch.

ALEX: A chicken in every pot.

CHRIS: Two cars in every garage.

ALEX: And two garages on every house.

CHRIS: We believe America belongs to Americans.

ALEX: We believe in an easier life.

CHRIS: A shorter workday.

ALEX: Higher pay.

CHRIS: Early retirement.

ALEX: An end to crime.

CHRIS: And disease.

ALEX: And dissent.

(KAREN pulls the gun out of her pocket.)

CHRIS: We believe in giving you what you want.

ALEX: In telling you what you want to hear.

CHRIS: In showing you what you want to see.

ALEX: We believe in a government--

CHRIS: --of Chris and Alex,

ALEX: by Chris and Alex,

CHRIS: for Chris and Alex.

ALEX: Under God's good name.

CHRIS: Amen. You can be important.

ALEX: You will be important. If you vote for us. Just never forget:

CHRIS & ALEX: Two Heads Are Better Than One.

(The crowd begins chanting, "Two Heads Are Better Than One.")

ALEX: Good night, America.

CHRIS: God Bless America.

(CHRIS and ALEX exit. The slide of the crowd blinks off. The cardboard cutout crowd is carted off stage. KAREN remains.)

KAREN: Their lives were mine for the taking. My hand was steady. Not a tremor. I knew the crowd would rip me to pieces, but I was not afraid of what they would do to me. I was afraid of creating martyrs, saints, Gods.

(KAREN exits. Lights up on JOLENE.)

67

JOLENE: Brothers and Sisters, I just wanted let you know that your generosity in our current fund drive has been unprecedented. With just a few more thousand dollars, we'll be able to buy those new sculptures of Chris and Alex for the front of our Church. I can't think of any better way to signal to the world our dedication to these holy men. Sister Martha has been compiling a collection of all their speeches and writings that we hope to publish soon, as the Gospel of Chris and Alex. We'll be looking for volunteers to head out in pairs to help spread the word, door to door. Amen.

NERVOUS BLADDER

(SOUND of a toilet flushing. ALEX enters, talking to someone off stage.)

ALEX: No. No. I've told you a hundred times, you are not coming in here with me. I am not going to get whacked in the bathroom. What is the matter with you? You want to see my pecker? You want to see my pecker? Good. Then stay out there until I'm done.

(ALEX walks over to a corner of the stage and, with his back to the audience, prepares to urinate. Nothing happens. He waits, whistles. Waits.)

(SOUND of a toilet flushing again. WILBUR and KAREN enter, quietly, unseen by ALEX. WILBUR produces a large strip of duct tape and suddenly tapes it across ALEX's mouth. They drag ALEX off stage, struggling.)

ON THE LOOKOUT

(The two SHOPPERS enter with their baskets/bags. Both wear elaborate Chris and Alex outfits.)

SHOPPER1:   Did you watch the Chris and Alex Network last night?

SHOPPER2: It's all I ever watch. I actually smashed the remote, so the channel never changes.

SHOPPER1: Did you hear about that woman--Karen Sayer?

SHOPPER2: Crazy psychopath. If Chris and Alex get elected, they won't let people like that escape.

SHOPPER1: I heard they might take all the crazies and wall them up in some big compound. Maybe Rhode Island.

SHOPPER2: How could anyone threaten Chris and Alex?

SHOPPER1: They're so sweet.

SHOPPER2: Innocent.

SHOPPER1: Pure.

SHOPPER2: And sexy.

SHOPPER1: I've got my stun gun.

SHOPPER2: Too good for the likes of her. You want something bloody and painful.

SHOPPER1: And public. Send a message.

SHOPPER2: I might have to buy some steel-toed boots. Just in case.

SHOPPER1: I think they're on sale over on Washington Street!

(SHOPPERS exit.)

STACK'S FIRST LIE

(Podium, projected crowd, cardboard cutout crowd. STACK suddenly appears at the podium.)

STACK: Ladies and gentlemen. It is time for the moment you've been waiting for. It is time for the split second that will change your reason for existence. Those of you who have been lost, have found a home. Tonight, you become part of the biggest movement in America. Tonight, YOU WILL BE PART OF CHRIS AND ALEX!

(Deafening applause and cheering. CHRIS emerges, alone. He waits, expectantly. Suddenly KAREN appears, dressed in Alex's suit. STACK seems unsure of what to do. KAREN and CHRIS shake his hand.)

STACK: Ladies and gentlemen... Chris and Alex!

(More cheering. CHRIS and KAREN stand by the podiums. STACK stands off to one side and watches, stricken.)

KAREN: Thank you, Stack.

CHRIS: And thanks to all of you--

KAREN: --for coming to listen--

CHRIS: --and to share--

KAREN: --what is important.

(Thunderous cheering.)

KAREN: Because what you think is important...

CHRIS: Is, uh, what we think is important.

KAREN: And that's why you can trust us to lead you,

CHRIS: To lead America,

KAREN: Wherever you want us to go.

CHRIS: Wherever WE want it to go.

(Loud cheers.)

KAREN: You may have seen some press conferences lately where reporters have asked what exactly do we stand for.

CHRIS: Questioning our programs.

VOICE IN CROWD: Lynch 'em!

KAREN: No, no. That's not the spirit of what we believe. We believe that questioning is good.

CHRIS: Reporters are our friends. Some are even here tonight.

(They wave and smile. Thousands of flash bulbs go off.)

KAREN: Stop, you sycophants.

CHRIS: Alex meant to say, stop, you respected members of the press.

(Flash bulbs stop.)

KAREN: Bloodsucking maggots.

CHRIS: That is meant in the best sense, of course. Now... uh, we want people... we're not afraid of hard questions.

71

KAREN: Of tough decisions.

CHRIS: Of making whatever choices we feel we have to.

KAREN: Especially if they're popular.

CHRIS: What do we stand for?

KAREN: We'll tell you.

CHRIS: Lower taxes.

(Loud cheers.)

KAREN: Actually, we can't afford lower taxes.

(The cheering stops.)

CHRIS: Free lunch.

KAREN: For the rich. The poor will have to go hungry.

CHRIS: We believe America belongs to Americans.

KAREN: As long as you're willing to be exploited.

CHRIS: We do not believe in exploitation.

KAREN: Chris has a secret.

CHRIS: I do not.

KAREN: I think you should share.

CHRIS: What the Hell--

(Loud fanfare of music. STACK rushes over to the podiums.)

STACK: Thank you Chris and Alex for that inspiring speech. (*Weak cheers.*) I can see that you're both exhausted after a grueling month on the road. Let's have a big cheer of support for our two champions. (*Louder cheers.*) We have a special reception for the press, and the sample vans are-- (*A RUNNER sprints on and gives Stack a note.*) (*reading to self*) On fire? (*to the Crowd*) The sample vans are temporarily unavailable tonight, (*a murmur runs through the crowd*) but we have plenty of T-shirts and videos. Please, take some home and help the cause. One more time, Chris and Alex!

(*Lukewarm cheers. The crowd and podiums are removed.*)

CHRIS: God Bless America... (*to Karen*) What was with you tonight, man?

KAREN: I was just being myself.

CHRIS: No you weren't, because I'm yourself and yourself definitely wasn't feeling like myself tonight.

KAREN: Maybe there's something wrong with you.

CHRIS: That wasn't our speech, Alex.

STACK: Chris, why don't you go to your room. I need to have a talk with Alex.

(*CHRIS exits.*)

STACK: What the hell are you doing?

KAREN: I don't know what you're talking about.

STACK: If anyone had recognized you, they would have killed you.

KAREN: They did recognize me. I'm Alex.

STACK: Karen.

KAREN: Why are you calling me Karen?

STACK: We have to get you out of here.

KAREN: I'm going to be President.

STACK: You can't keep it up, Karen.

KAREN: You laid the groundwork, Stack. Sixty thousand people just accepted me as Alex. Well done.

STACK: What have you done with my candidate?

KAREN: T.U.M.O.T.S.C.A.F.R.O.P. has him.

STACK: I want him back.

KAREN: I'm afraid I can't do that.

STACK: You want to be President?

KAREN: I want you to tell the truth.

STACK: The first time I ever told a lie in my life was when I introduced you as Alex.

KAREN: You knew they weren't the same.

STACK: I never looked that closely.

KAREN: Save it for your public.

STACK: I can mass market inferiority and unhappiness, but people don't want to feel idiotic.

KAREN: I have a month for Alex to lose this election. A slip-up here, a slip-up there. Tonight was just an appetizer.

STACK: You'll merely be exposed as Karen Sayer, as the murderer of Alex. When that happens, there will be a thousand Jack Ruby wannabes lined up around the block, waiting to put a bullet in your gut.

KAREN: Will you expose me?

STACK: Give me Alex.

KAREN: Or you'll have me ripped to pieces?

STACK: (*beat*) God, I love you.

KAREN: Please don't.

STACK: No one else would risk her life like this. No one else would make the commitment. That's what we have in common, you and I, the ability to commit our resources one hundred percent. No half measures.

KAREN: You didn't used to be like this, Stack.

STACK: I was always like this.

KAREN: I loved you.

STACK: Maybe you're not as different from everyone else as you want to be. Some things you see, some things you don't. That's how relationships work.

KAREN: This is not about us. Have you even listened to the message that your puppets are spouting?

STACK: I admit that they've become harsher than I intended. A tad out of control. But people buy it. I am good at what I do, Karen. When they want something different, I will give it to them. But as long as they lap it up, gulp it down, baying like hounds chasing the fox... This is the ultimate deal, the biggest game in the world. And I'm not just playing, I'm winning. I'm not just winning, I'm cleaning up. Most people never get a chance like this in their entire lives, or if they do, they blow it. Not me.

KAREN: But you are. Don't you get it? You're selling them junk. That's never what you were about. You believed in what you sold, because there was some basis of fact in it, there was some good. Do you think you're really accomplishing something if you seal this deal? What will you have won? It's not a challenge to sell someone a gold covered turd. They like the sparkle, the shine. You say you want a challenge, get them to buy something that's good for them, even if it tastes bad. You have the ability, Stack. Your customers deserve better than this. America deserves the truth.

STACK: There is no truth.

KAREN: I am not Alex. Alex is not Chris.

STACK: If no one sees it, how do you know it's true?

KAREN: I see it.

STACK: What do you see in our distinguished opponent, Senator Caldwell? Is he a well-adjusted Senator, fighting the good fight? Or a corrupt, corporate lap dog, a cigar smoking, intern shagging, pill popping, pillar of society? He's rotten to the core. Do you think he's the right choice?

KAREN: Listen to Chris and Alex's campaign message, and you'll understand the difference.

STACK: I was listening tonight. And I heard a change. A softening of tone. A sudden chord of reason... You're right. Our message can evolve. Show me the way. You've always had a better sense for what's right and what's wrong. You know. Two heads are better than one... if one of them is yours.

KAREN: I do not want to be President. I am here to put an end to this charade. That is the only reason.

STACK: Who better to take us back to reality and justice? Your vision is clear. You owe it to The People to lead the way. That's all I'm saying. You have a responsibility.

KAREN: To present the truth.

STACK: Think about what you can accomplish... See you at our breakfast meeting tomorrow, Alex.

(STACK exits.)

KAREN: The important thing with Stack is never to believe a word he says. I keep telling myself... He's not right. I know my responsibility. No doubt. I just have to wait for the right moment. It's like demolishing a building. You don't have to blow up the whole thing, you just need to shatter the right supports. He can't be right. He can't be.

BREAKFAST OF CHAMPIONS

(KAREN is joined by CHRIS.)

CHRIS: Morning, Alex. Feeling good?

KAREN: Never better.

CHRIS: I thought so. Can't wait for the debate tonight.

KAREN: Me neither.

CHRIS: Of course. That Caldwell is real weasel.

KAREN: Without a doubt. A total--

CHRIS: Slimeball.

KAREN: We'll bury him. Because he--

CHRIS: --doesn't know what the people--

KAREN: --want. What they need.

CHRIS: We can show them.

KAREN: Enlighten them.

CHRIS: Train them.

KAREN: Control them.

CHRIS: Lead them by their chain link--

KAREN: --collars.

CHRIS: Exactly.

KAREN: But I've been thinking.

CHRIS: Have we? I thought Stack warned us against--

KAREN: --speculation. I'm sure he did. But this time
we've just had a little--

CHRIS: --brainstorm?

KAREN: Just that we might want to ask a few more questions. Of the People. Before we lead.

CHRIS: Interesting. I didn't realize I'd been thinking that.

KAREN: You should.

CHRIS: Of course. But I'm hungry for breakfast. Shall we?

KAREN: I think so.

CHRIS: Here, pig, pig, pig, pig. Let 'em loose, Stack.

(STACK enters with two people in jackets and ties and plastic pig noses. Maybe even some curly pig tails on their pants. Both carry bulging sacks.)

STACK: Greetings, boys. You look radiant this morning, Alex.

KAREN: Thanks.

STACK: We have some distinguished guests for breakfast this morning. This is Horace Greenstone, from the United Union of Autoworkers and Railsplitters.

HOG-1: It's an honor to meet you both. I know our membership is extremely eager for your election. "Two Cars in Every Garage."

CHRIS: How eager?

(HOG-1 opens his bag and shows CHRIS and KAREN the contents.)

KAREN: That's pretty illegal, I mean, eager.

STACK: I understand that you and the missus would like an entire week in the Lincoln bedroom.

CHRIS: Do you have a picture of her?

79

(HOG-1 pulls out his wallet and shows CHRIS.)

CHRIS: Sweet. Maybe we'll join you.

STACK: Just add the bag to the pile and help yourself to a croissant, friend.

(HOG-1 exits with bag. The next person in line, HOG-2, steps forward.)

STACK: Presenting Ned Raferty, CEO of American Petroleum and Chemical.

KAREN: I know you. The Chlorine Kid. I wrote a...

HOG-2: No one ever proved that leak was our fault.

KAREN: But--

STACK: The real problem is an excess of regulation. Wouldn't you say?

HOG-2: Oh, I definitely would.

CHRIS: Me, too.

STACK: Alex?

KAREN: You know my answer.

STACK: Of course we do. Now let's see if Ned understands the difficulty of eliminating said regulations.

(HOG-2 opens his bag.)

CHRIS: You are a very understanding man.

HOG-2: We like to do things right at my company.

STACK: I'm sure you do... But maybe you can explain to Alex about your visit to Senator Caldwell.

HOG-2: (*suddenly nervous*) Excuse me?

STACK: Before our campaign really hit its stride. My understanding is that you brought a little donation to Caldwell's campaign.

HOG-2: You know how it is. I just try to make sure that good people get elected, and if they do... that they remember to do good things when they're in office.

CHRIS: I suddenly feel dirty.

HOG-2: You understand. It was a formality. A business decision. Common practice. I hadn't come to see the light. There's so much that I didn't understand. It was nothing like this. Not nearly as much. You have to believe me.

CHRIS: Why, just look at my shoes. I can't keep them clean. I must have stepped in something. So many hogs running about.

STACK: Perhaps Mr. Raferty could help.

CHRIS: I'm sure.

(*HOG-2 pulls out a handkerchief.*)

CHRIS: Unacceptable. Tongue.

HOG-2: But...

STACK: Please, Mr. Raferty. Breakfast is waiting.

(*HOG-2 licks CHRIS's shoes clean. KAREN is stunned.*)

CHRIS: Not a speck left. Well done, hog. Leave us.

(HOG-2 exits.)

KAREN: Thank you for the illustration, Stack. Very informative.

STACK: You can be a catalyst for change, Alex. That's what we're all about, isn't it, Chris?

CHRIS: Changing the world.

STACK: Think about it, Alex. Think about how you can change the world. Let's eat.

(ALL exit.)

THE DEBATE

(The MODERATOR enters, carrying a clipboard. Perhaps he has an earphone in one ear. He walks to the center of the stage. House lights up.)

MODERATOR: Welcome to our last televised debate between the candidates for Presidents of the United States. Before we begin, let's cover a few ground rules. Because of the well-deserved popularity of two of our candidates, you might have the impulse to leap out of your seats, strip naked, and offer yourselves body and soul. Please restrain yourselves. Also do not touch, kiss, or ask difficult questions of our leaders. As for the challenger, I suppose we should also respect him, so no tripping, eye-gouging, or spitting. Let's bring out our dynamic duo, twenty-five point leaders in the polls, recently named Most Beautiful Men of the Century by People Magazine. The two, the only, Chris and Alex. *(Very loud applause and cheering. CHRIS and KAREN enter and wave triumphantly. STACK enters quietly*

82

behind them.) And next, our challenger, an eighteen-year veteran of our increasingly corrupt Senate, investigated seventeen times by the ethics committee, veteran of two sex scandals and an accusation of bribery, Senator Tax and Spend Caldwell. *(SENATOR CALDWELL enters to a chorus of boos. He does not look happy.)* Chris and Alex, I just want to say that it's an honor to have you here. Your opening statement please.

CHRIS: Thank you for your generous introduction.

KAREN: And thank you America, for listening to what we have to say.

CHRIS: Because never has it been more important--

KAREN: that you listen, carefully.

CHRIS: About what we'll do.

KAREN: For you.

CHRIS: And for us. We plan to bring prosperity,

KAREN: happiness

CHRIS: obedience

KAREN: justice

CHRIS: conformity

KAREN: freedom

CHRIS: complacency

KAREN: but most of all we just want you to listen tonight. We might have a surprise.

CHRIS: Not really. You know what to expect, America. You expect us to lead you where we want to go. Pay attention and do as you're told. Simple. Our message is very simple. God Bless America.

MODERATOR: Stunning, as usual. Senator Caldwell, dare you follow that opening?

SENATOR CALDWELL: I am not a bad man. Do you understand that? Despite the vicious, completely false attack ads run by my opponents, I will not sink to calling them filthy despotic liars, I will not call them spawn of hell. But I do want America to pay attention and see that these goons are twisting what little we have left of--

MODERATOR: Thank you, Senator.

SENATOR CALDWELL: But I--

MODERATOR: Time for our first audience question. (*looks at his clipboard*) Judy, from Saranac Lake, New York. Can you please stand up and give us your question?

(*JUDY, a nervous spectator stands up and reads from a sheet of paper.*)

JUDY: Hi. This... this is for Chris and Alex. I just have to say that I'm an incredible fan. I have your entire porcelain statuette collection, and I've watched the video of your speech at the Great Mall of America one hundred and fifty three times.

CHRIS: You're a good citizen, Judy.

MODERATOR: The question, please.

JUDY: Oh, right. I'm just like, you know, so... So I was wondering. My question has two parts. First, I wanted to know... Do you wear boxes or briefs? And can you please explain your economic plan for America?

CHRIS: We wear boxers. The first thing we need to do is to make Americans richer.

KAREN: With a closer look at our economy--

CHRIS: --you'll see that we especially need to make rich Americans richer.

KAREN: This has always been one of our strengths as a country. But we also need to find a way to deal with poverty.

CHRIS: We hate poverty.

KAREN: But we--

CHRIS: --also hate the poor. The easiest way to get rid of them--

KAREN: We really want to help them.

CHRIS: --is by locking them up. In our America, there will be no more poor people.

KAREN: No, what I'm trying to say is--

CHRIS: Thanks for asking that important question.

MODERATOR: Okay, our next question will be from--

SENATOR CALDWELL: Don't I get a response?

MODERATOR: Are you still here?

SENATOR CALDWELL: Now just a minute, I have been subjected to a lot of--

MODERATOR: Your indignation is duly noted. But we have Americans with questions to ask, Senator. James from Buena Vista, Colorado. Where are you?

(JAMES stands, ready to go.)

JAMES: I have a question for Senator Caldwell.

SENATOR CALDWELL: Go ahead, James, I'm listening.

JAMES: What characteristics best qualify Chris and Alex for the presidency?

SENATOR CALDWELL: Although they are both completely ignorant of the workings of government, economics, and foreign affairs, they possess a grotesque charm which allows people to see past their shortcomings. This would qualify them to be elected, but not actually to be President. This charm can not last forever.

MODERATOR: Chris and Alex, your response.

CHRIS: Bite me.

KAREN: Actually, what Chris means is that we're fast learners. We've been fast learning about corruption in your campaign, Senator. Millions of dollars in illegal campaign contributions. We have witnesses.

SENATOR CALDWELL: Lies, lies, lies. I will not stand for any more lies from you people.

CHRIS: *(to audience, trying to start a chant)* Chris and Alex. Chris and Alex. Chris and Alex.

SENATOR CALDWELL: When will you start telling the truth to the American people? How can you look at yourselves in the mirror? You have taken what little sanity we had and turned it inside out. Do you think this is right? Do you think this is right?

KAREN: Senator Caldwell, for once I agree. Your campaign is not the only corrupt one. We have told a few lies of our own.

STACK: (*calling out from the sidelines*) Alex!

CHRIS: We have never told lies. Only the truth. (*to Caldwell*) And I have one word for you, you perverted, twisted, sick old bastard.

(KAREN starts unbuttoning her shirt and jacket.)

KAREN: I am ready to tell America the truth about myself. To show you that I am not what I seem.

CHRIS: Rosebud.

SENATOR CALDWELL: That's it! That's it! You scum-sucking demon from Hell!

(SENATOR CALDWELL produces a pistol from his jacket.)

KAREN: I have been part of this lie. But the truth is that I'm really--

JAMES: He's got a gun!

(SENATOR CALDWELL shoots CHRIS.)

CHRIS: I'm shot.

(CHRIS dies. CALDWELL turns the gun on KAREN, but STACK runs across the stage and tackles SENATOR CALDWELL.)

STACK: Get her out of here!

(The MODERATOR pulls KAREN off stage. JUDY and JAMES join STACK in brutally subduing SENATOR CALDWELL, and then drag him off stage.)

AFTERMATH

(The SHOPPERS.)

SHOPPER1: Are you going to vote?

SHOPPER2: Of course. After what happened, it's never been more important.

SHOPPER1: That's what Oprah says, anyway. If you ask me, society has gone to Hell.

SHOPPER2: Murder. Lies. Corruption.

SHOPPER1: Thank God I got to see it on TV. The replay was really something.

SHOPPER2: Oh, I taped it.

SHOPPER1: I haven't voted for anything since Homecoming Queen.

SHOPPER2: Always a blonde.

SHOPPER1: Natural order of things.

SHOPPER2: Do you think I should color my hair?

(THEY exit.)

DECISION

(Backstage at the inauguration, behind a small piece of velvet curtain on a rod. On the other side a podium and cardboard cut-out crowd are being installed, along with a pair of empty folding chairs. We're outside on a bright winter's morning.)

(KAREN, in her Alex suit, waits to go on stage, a little nervous.)

(WILBUR JENKINS appears, in his fedora and overcoat, looking around carefully.)

KAREN: Wilbur! Wilbur, get over here. Where have you been?

WILBUR: T.U.M.O.T.S.K.I.R.O.P. has been checking out the area. You're still in a dangerous position.

KAREN: You don't have to sneak around anymore, remember? And I thought it was Tumotscafrop, not Tumotskirop.

WILBUR: We've obviously had to change our name and mission, given the nature of reality. We are now The Underground Movement Operating To Support Karen In Ruling Our Planet.

KAREN: I see. Well, I'm glad you're on my side.

WILBUR: We will give our lives to protect you from exposure, Karen. You saved us from the menace, you risked everything, you have the capacity to take us to a new level of moral responsibility and truth. We believe in you, Karen.

KAREN: I still wish there was another way.

(STACK enters, with FLOYD and WANDA.)

STACK: We don't have much time, but I wanted you to meet them before things started.

WANDA: Oh, Lord, we've just never been at anything like this before.

FLOYD: See, this is what connections can do for a person. We're lucky to know you, Stack.

(They stop in front of KAREN and WILBUR. FLOYD and WANDA are all a twitter, meeting real celebrities and all.)

STACK: First, I'd like you to meet Wilbur Jenkins, vice-president elect.

(They shake hands.)

FLOYD: I want to say that it is a true honor to meet you, Mr. Vice President.

WILBUR: No. The honor is all mine. What you two have given to our country... I barely can find the words... You will be honored by history.

(He's nearly overcome with emotion at having met this "holy" family.)

WANDA: *(in a loud whisper to Floyd)* They say Washington is all about flattery.

STACK: And this is President-Elect Alex.

WANDA: Oh, my word. Should I curtsey?

KAREN: Definitely not.

FLOYD: We've been big supporters, followers, for, well, practically as long as we can remember.

WANDA: If we were to have grandchildren, which, sadly, I fear we never may, we would tell them this was the most exciting moment of our entire lives.

FLOYD: Alex, in the flesh.

KAREN: Thanks for coming. It... means a lot to me.

FLOYD: We're just ordinary folks.

KAREN: To me, you seem like family.

FLOYD: That's so kind. Family, they can make you or break you, I always say.

WANDA: Don't you get started, Floyd. We've had a little trouble with our daughter.

KAREN: I'm sure she'll be fine.

WANDA: They tell us she's in a safe place now, and that the medication is working.

STACK: Well, folks, it looks like we're about ready to start. I'll have an usher take you to your seats.

(He raises his hand, and ALEX runs on--he's an usher now, greatly subdued in personality, not so sharply dressed as before, perhaps in a baseball cap.)

STACK: Son, can you take these folks to their seats?

ALEX: Yes, sir.

FLOYD: First class, all the way.

91

(ALEX takes FLOYD and WANDA to their seats in the empty folding chairs, then exits.)

KAREN: What the... That was Alex!

WILBUR: He's one of us now. We've had a team working with him around the clock. He was incredibly malleable. He's one of your biggest supporters now.

KAREN: I don't know if I can do this.

STACK: Excuse us for a second, Wilbur. *(STACK takes KAREN aside.)* Now is not the time for cold feet, Karen. You have the talent, the responsibility, even the support. You must go forward. This is The Moment. Look at those people out there--they are eager customers. They just want you to tell them that they made the right purchase. You won't be stranded--I'll be by your side. We've been through a lot together, and to me you're... We're more than just a team, more than just a couple. You know we are.

KAREN: About that--

STACK: I know what you're thinking. *(He reaches into his pocket and produces a ring box.)* I should have asked a long time ago. Marry me, Karen.

KAREN: Stack, somewhere deep inside you is a dear, sweet man. I'm sure of it. But I can't marry you. For one thing, officially, I'm a man. The country just isn't ready for a gay married president, even if I really am a woman. Secondly, and I've given this a lot of thought, really considered all that you've done during the campaign and even in our relationship. Most of all, I've been thinking about what it would mean to have your influence on the country as my chief of staff. You've already done so much.

STACK: It's a gift, really.

KAREN: Which is why, in two hours, you will leave for Uzbekistan, as my new ambassador.

(ALEX, still as usher, runs up.)

ALEX: They're ready now, Mr. President.

(ALEX exits. KAREN reaches out and grabs STACK by the hand and shakes it vigorously. WILBUR comes over to them.)

KAREN: Goodbye, Stack.

STACK: Karen...

WILBUR: It's time.

(KAREN and WILBUR walk out to the podium, where they are joined by a black-robed CHIEF JUSTICE, with a bible in one hand. The CHIEF JUSTICE extends the bible, and KAREN places her left hand on it and raises her right.)

CHIEF JUSTICE: Repeat after me. I do solemnly swear that I will faithfully execute the Office of the President of the United States...

KAREN: I do solemnly swear that I will faithfully execute the Office of the President of the United States...

CHIEF JUSTICE: and will to the best of my ability, preserve, protect, and defend the constitution of the United States.

KAREN: and will to the best of my ability, preserve, protect, and defend the constitution of the United States.

(Thunderous applause. The CHIEF JUSTICE steps away, leaving KAREN alone at the podium.)

KAREN: Mr. Chief Justice, Vice President Wilbur Jenkins, my fellow Americans. We're here today because... well, because the world, on the surface, or under the surface, doesn't always make sense. My running mate is dead, my opponent is in jail, and I am here. I don't want to be here. I don't think it's right. But then, I look out and I see... I see ordinary Americans, like Floyd and Wanda Sayer. Stand up, Floyd and Wanda. *(FLOYD and WANDA stand nervously to acknowledge applause and then take their seats again.)* They have been avid supporters of me and Chris, willing to make incredible sacrifices. Because they wanted to believe--they had faith that deep down they were being told the truth by the people in authority. In the face of the facts, and I mean cold, hard data, presented to them by their own daughter, they refused to waver. Should they be applauded? Praised? Forgiven? The notion of truthfulness in our leaders is rooted in the American myth. George Washington's cherry tree, Lincoln walking miles to return a forgotten penny. And that's what I want. The truth, truthfulness. But also about them, about me. Isn't that what you deserve? But the truth is that there was no cherry tree, no overlooked penny. And as for me... I will follow their paths and attempt to lead, to forge something good from the hidden, seething machine that has brought me to this point. You have called upon me, whoever that may be, for leadership, for a commitment to truth and justice. If that's not exactly what you asked for, that's what I will attempt to provide. God bless America.

(She concludes. There is enthusiastic applause. FLOYD and WANDA lead a standing ovation.)

(KAREN waves to the crowd as the lights fade.)

THE END.

NOTES

NOTES

NOTES

NOTES

Made in the USA
Middletown, DE
18 March 2024

51156433R00056